EFFECTIVE

MANAGEMENT

IN THE

PUBLIC SERVICE

EFFECTIVE

MANAGEMENT

IN THE

PUBLIC SERVICE

by Jeremy Thorn

The Industrial Society

First published 1983 by
The Industrial Society
Peter Runge House
3 Carlton House Terrace
London SW1Y 5DG
Telephone: 01–839 4300

Second edition 1989

ISBN 0 85290 430 4

British Library Cataloguing in Publication Data
Thorn, Jeremy
  Effective management in the public service. — 2nd ed.
  1. Public sector. Management
  I. Title   II. Industrial Society   III. Series
  350

Typeset by Columns Ltd, Reading
Printed and bound in Great Britain by Belmont Press, Northampton

CONTENTS

FOREWORD

Whatever the discipline or level of management, the responsibilities of a manager are many and various. It is their job to produce results with essentially just two resources—people and time.

To maximise the potential of both, most managers need some reminders and basic guidelines to help them.

The Notes for Managers series provides succinct yet comprehensive coverage of key management issues and skills. The short time it takes to read each title will pay dividends in terms of utilising one of those key resources—people.

The Public Service is the biggest employer in the country. As such, it is an important subject for study. This short book outlines in straightforward terms the very simple actions that managers in the public service need to take in order to get the best out of their people and develop their managerial skills for the benefit of the community in which we all live.

ALISTAIR GRAHAM
Director, The Industrial Society

1

WHO'S IN CHARGE?

Structure of working groups

Structures in the public services tend to be more complex than in industry or commerce. Sometimes this takes the form of a multiplicity of tiers and a profusion of deputies (as, often, in local government). In many cases, members of separately organised groups work side-by-side (as, most obviously, in the hospital service). There are often valid reasons for such methods of working, but experience of other organisations suggests that an unclear structure can seriously impair effectiveness.

By simplifying, it is possible to improve the speed and accuracy of communication and ensure that people are clearer about the contribution expected from them. On a local level, managers can make sure their own teams know who is in charge of what.

Accountability

To be helpful, structure should not be a matter of status or vertical position on a structure chart, but, rather, a matter of who is accountable for the work of other staff. This is particularly critical where ambiguity exists as, for instance, where there is both a professional boss and a senior administration officer in one unit. Who is the clerical officer's boss in this case? The answer will, of course, vary with circumstances, but that answer must be clear and understood by all staff. If it appears that there are two 'thick line' bosses there will, inevitably, be confusion in priorities. 'Dotted line' relationships must, of course, be present in any sophisticated organisation. What is important is that everyone knows where the thick line is.

In an organisation with clear structure and accountability, any member of staff should be able to answer the question: 'Who is your boss?' rapidly and with one name. Some examples of Accountability Charts are shown in the Appendix, in each case showing the thick line relationship, irrespective of status.

The manager as a leader

It is not sufficient to know who is in charge. Those in charge must also know what to do. Most early career development in the public services is based on technical or professional skills and knowledge. However, in almost all careers, people will become responsible for the work of others. At that point, technical expertise will not be enough. Those in charge must discover what action to take to get the best out of their people.

The leader of any working team is responsible for:

● achieving the task
● building the team
● developing individuals.

Any action taken in one of these areas will affect at least one of the others. For example, disciplinary action involving one individual will almost always influence the attitude of the rest of the team and the amount and quality of work done.

A team that loses sight of its task will be unlikely to achieve it. If they are never brought together they will not co-operate effectively. If individuals are ignored or over-favoured, the team's work will be impaired.

By no means all of these responsibilites will be self-evident to newly-appointed bosses. People need advice and instruction in what leaders do. In 12 to 16 hours, it is possible to train all leaders, in a practical way, to understand these actions.

2

In particular, those in charge must:

- understand the tasks they are responsible for
- share the commitment with their team
- clarify the task for each individual
- decide set standards and priorities
- structure teams in the most effective way for getting the work done
- consult before they decide
- delegate to individuals and set targets
- regularly brief their teams
- walk round all places of work; observe and listen
- praise good work, pass on thanks to individuals
- monitor standards of work and discipline
- Co-ordinate and reconcile conflict
- advise, reassure and counsel individuals
- evaluate progress and replan if necessary
- learn from success and failure
- appraise, guide and train individuals.

Leadership, especially at the first line, is central to the success of any organisation because it directly affects those on the 'ground floor'. It is the amount and quality of work done by these people that decides the quantity and quality of the services provided.

Checklist of action

1 Simplify structure wherever possible. Make leaders accountable for groups of 15 or less.
2 If ambiguity exists, sort it out at local level.
3 Train leaders to achieve the task, build the team and develop individuals.

2

IMPROVING PERFORMANCE

Motivation

Motivation has been the subject of much theorising. For most managers, however, it is of the utmost practical importance. The difference between poorly and well motivated people can be seen in levels of absenteeism, in willingness to take on extra responsibility, in attitude to the public, but most of all in the work itself.

The first point about motivation is that is is individual; in other words, to motivate somebody you have to know that person and their needs and aspirations. Some general principles, however, seem to apply to a lot of people. Most people respond to wider responsibility, to achievement, to the recognition of that achievement, to growth and to promotion. Whilst physical factors such as money, working conditions, or status are important, they seem to have a negative effect more often than a positive one. The job of the manager, therefore, is:

- to increase the responsibility and achievement available to staff by delegating larger and higher-level-areas of work
- to ensure that good performance receives adequate thanks
- to develop staff so that their jobs expand in interest and worth, and promotion is more likely.

At the same time any action that can be taken to improve working conditions, to make salary more equitable, to consult and to explain decisions more, and, in general, to treat people better, will make people more open to motivation.

We can, sometimes, concentrate too much on the extremes. The totally unmotivated person may never respond. The already well-motivated do not need to. It is with the 80 per cent in the middle that we have most chance of success.

Staff development

Organisations need to develop staff in order to have more people more able to do more things, either now or in the future. By doing so they can be more cost-effective by 'growing' their future senior staff, by reducing recruitment and initial training costs, by covering absences or changes in staff better, and by generating more useful ideas. Individuals respond to development because it gives them opportunities for achievement, for broadening their skills and knowledge and, in some cases, for advancement.

A development plan is required, and this should aim to ensure that all staff know the following.

- Who is their boss? Future plans and priorities must be discussed with an individual who has the authority to decide.

- What is their job? This does not mean a detailed breakdown of all tasks, but a simple statement of the major areas of achievement expected.

- What standard is expected? Objective means are required to measure or recognise what level of perfor-mance has been achieved.

- How are they getting on? A regular (normally annual) review of development is vital to ensure that organisations and individuals develop in compatible directions. This must be a two-way, well prepared discussion.

- Where are they going in the future? What future work

and training is right for the organisation and the individual?

- How do they get there? What are the short-term priorities and targets?

Targets

The term 'target' is used with a variety of meanings in different contexts. In this case it means a precise goal set against a specific time-scale for an individual member of staff. Where possible, agreement should be sought between boss and job-holder as to the target itself and the time-scale but, in the end, it is the job of the manager to set the target. Targets may be:

- *one-off tasks with starting and finishing dates*, e.g. the completion of annual statistics, the production of a report, the holiday plan for the year

- *job improvement projects*, e.g. to develop a new duty rota, to incorporate a new approach to therapy in the work of a hospital ward, to change the method of working to allow for new legislation

- *to raise flagging standards within time limits*, e.g. to improve time-keeping over a set period, to reduce the level of public complaints, to ensure that all enquiries are responded to within a specific number of days

- *short-term investigations*, e.g. to examine and report on the possibility of introducing new technology, to find out what went wrong in a particular case, to find out what training exists in a new field

- *for personal development*, e.g. to learn shorthand, to take on a new aspect of work which will contribute to career development, to sit in with a more experienced colleague.

When setting targets it is vital to consider the following.

- **How many?** People will not work well at a vast list of targets but need enough to provide an element of challenge in their work.

- **For what period?** The time-scale must be attainable. It is best to avoid using the same date for several targets as this may make it more difficult for job-holders to organise their priorities.

- **How easily achieved?** A target should stretch the job-holder within achievable limits.

- **How precise?** A target must be exact in nature and in time-scale. Both parties need to be able to measure the degree of success.

- **How subject to alteration?** Long-term targets, particularly investigative ones, will require interim checks and, possibly, revision.

Planning induction and training

The most significant working day of anyone's life is the first. In that day we start to form many of the attitudes that we will carry with us throughout our careers. To a slightly lesser extent the same will be true of our first few weeks, and of starting in subsequent jobs. Induction is, therefore, an important managerial tool.

Clearly there are administrative tasks to be dealt with when new employees start. More importantly, it is the chance to begin the relationship between the line manager and the new employee on the right footing. Some simple actions flow from this realisation:

- ensuring that people are briefed on the new arrival
- the boss being available and meeting the recruit *before* the personnel department does

- spending time explaining the contribution of the job and of the section or department
- making sure that there is an induction plan
- providing working space and appropriate resources.

The new member of staff needs to know who is in charge and that they have access to help and guidance.

The continuation of training is also the manager's business. However sophisticated training departments may be, in the end most learning takes place 'on the job' and 'off the job' training is only of value if it helps with the work itself. The manager needs to both plan and record training. Such records should include significant learning by experience as well as formal training and should, of course, be related to the review of each person's overall development. It may also be helpful for the manager, and perhaps other trainers in their team, to receive training in instructional techniques.

Developing young employees

All employers have a special responsibility towards their younger employees. Firstly, the young represent the most important investment in the future (bearing in mind that, in all the major public services, more than half of expenditure is on staff). Secondly, they offer the opportunity to influence attitudes and exploit talents at an early stage.

It is worth remembering that the young seem to have changed in recent years; there is no longer an automatic respect for seniority. Young people have been educated to question, and to regard their own ideas as importantly as those of their elders. It is fruitless for the manager to bemoan such changes. The job of the manager is to recognise the reality by clarifying working standards and disciplines for young people, while at the same time encouraging the willingness to contribute ideas.

Planned induction and systematic training are of particular significance for young people. Much of what they are learning is about the working world in general as well as their particular job and place of work, so greater care about the detail of induction will be required. This, of course, often applies as much to the graduate as to the 16-year-old. Work is different from education and it is a function of management to explain the difference.

Making decisions and managing time

The manager's own performance is often dependant on the ability to control both personal professional duties and managerial responsibilities. This requires a disciplined approach to controlling the use of time and to decision-making. 'There's never enough time' actually means we must decide what *not* to do and we must ensure that our decisions are clear and well understood so as not to waste time.

To take effective decisions we must:

consider—the time scale of the decision, the background, the implications
consult—all those affected by the decision
crunch—make the decision clearly and promptly; if marginal take the courageous course
communicate—inform all those who have to carry out, or are affected by, the decision
check—monitor to make sure the decision has been carried out and that it works.

To improve our use of time we can:

- check our current use of time with a simple time log
- categorise tasks by priority and devote time to high priority tasks
- establish a 'brought forward' system in which work is allocated to a specific time in the future when it will be dealt with
- handle paper once—take some action immediately, even if that is simply allocating a time to it

- control interruptions
- work at one job at a time.

Checklist of action

1 Get to know staff, delegate more, recognise effort.
2 Set objective standards and targets; review them regularly.
3 Have an induction checklist; plan and monitor training.
4 Make special efforts to develop young employees.
5 Take action to make decisions promptly and to consult, inform and monitor their effect.
6 Use time on high-priority tasks.

3

COMMUNICATION

Methods

There are three main methods of communication available at work:

oral—informal and formal meetings and interviews, the telephone, casual conversations, tapes, etc.
written—letters, memos, reports, books, noticeboards, etc.
visual—non verbal signs, colours, diagrams, gestures, facial expressions, etc.

Visual communication at work is almost always used as a support for speech or writing (e.g. a diagram in a book, or a visual aid with a lecture).

Barriers

Written communication is the most fallible. Firstly, there is no guarantee that it has reached the right destination. Secondly, there is no guarantee that it has been read (noticeboards and circulation systems are obvious examples). Thirdly, there is no guarantee that it has been understood. (One cannot, of course, ask questions of a memo.)
   Oral communication is much more immediate and personal but suffers from lack of permanence. In particular, records may be needed for legal or procedural reasons.
   For effective communication, therefore, the rule is to speak, then to back up in writing.

Establishing regular communication drills

The greatest difficulty with communication is making it happen. There is a need, therefore, for a systematic drill. Most managers will express a pious intention to let people know all they need to know; it will remain an intention unless a forum exists for communication. This should be:

- face-to-face so that questions can be put
- in small groups of similar status—to remove inhibitions due to difference in status and small enough to encourage involvement by everybody
- regular and at a set time booked ahead in diaries—people come to trust regular communications
- brief—a useful half hour will make people want to attend, while a rambled three hours will not
- relevant—above all, communication at work should be concerned with matters of direct influence on those involved.

This approach may operate in various ways.

- **Lateral**. In complex organisations it is often better to have a regular inter-departmental meeting than to rely on *ad hoc* contacts. Misunderstanding and mistrust will always accompany a failure to communicate effectively.

- **Downwards**. It is the responsibility of each manager to make sure that his or her own team are briefed about:
  - *policy*—particularly changes that affect the team's work
  - *people*—who's new, who's left, who's got new responsibilities?
  - *progress*—how are things going, what significant events have happened?
  - *points for action*—what particular things need priority now? This becomes even more important when organisation change is taking place.

If we, ourselves, are unclear about these things, then there are two resulting actions. Firstly, share what we *do* know; secondly, try to find out more before our next briefing.

- **Upwards**. There are two important reasons for consulting. In the first place, managers do not have a monopoly of expertise so they need the help of their staff. In the second place, people tend to feel more committed to a decision they have had a chance to comment on. Consultation does not, of course, mean automatic acceptance of those comments. It simply means a willingness to listen before taking the decision.

Chairing meetings more effectively

Public service managers will spend more time in meetings than most of their counterparts in industry and commerce. It is important, therefore, that these meetings are as productive as possible. Our best chance to influence this is when we are in the chair. To chair effectively we must carry out the following.

Prepare. Be sure of the objective(s) of the meeting; is a meeting the best way of reaching these objectives? Get the right people there and leave out people who will have nothing to contribute; invite particular people for one agenda item if their presence would be irrelevant for the rest of the meeting.

Plan and write an agenda which informs people of what is to be discussed and why (one word items will only cause confusion). Plan the time needed for each item, and therefore, the whole meeting.

Appoint a note-taker or minute-taker (decide which; relatively few meetings require verbatim minutes).
Make sure that the room is booked, suitably laid out and that, if appropriate, refreshments are available.

Conduct. Start on time—it is a discourtesy to those already there to delay for one or two latecomers.

Involve everybody. Take action to bring out the shy, reserved or new. Politely but firmly shut up the loquacious and irrelevant. Ask open questions.

Control. All contributions must be through the chair. Make clear opening statements and summarise at the end of each item. Always identify what action will be taken by whom by when.

Summarise decisions and resulting action at the end and thank people for their attendance.

Follow up. Ensure that minutes or notes are written and distributed promptly.

Check that agreed action has taken place by the agreed date.

Evaluate the meeting—did it work? Was the discussion always relevant? Did everybody have a chance to contribute?

Interviewing staff, applicants and the public

'Interview' is a rather formal word that we often reserve for formal events. All it means, however, is a conversation with a purpose (normally it also implies a one-to-one conversation, but 'panel' interviews are an exception). If, to formal interviews, we add the less formal occasions on which we have discussions with staff, colleagues or the public, we can see that interviewing is one of the main ways in which we manage. It is thus important to derive as much benefit from interviews as is possible. We can help towards this end by undertaking the following.

- Doing our homework; getting the facts right before we start (sometimes this will also mean checking law or procedure, as, for instance, in a disciplinary interview).
- Allowing the right amount of time; if people feel rushed they will not co-operate as well as they might.

- Finding the right place; privacy is normally a prerequisite of interviews. Action may have to be taken to control interruptions. An informal layout of the room may help to encourage open discussion.
- In a panel interview, making sure that each member of the panel understands their role beforehand.
- Clarifying objectives; make sure the interviewee understands the purpose of the discussion and of each section of it.
- Asking open questions; that is, questions that do not require 'yes' or 'no' answers. Prepare a few of these questions—they are sometimes difficult to come up with in mid-discussion.
- Summarising at the end of each area of discussion and at the very end. This gives us a chance to check mutual understanding and to record and avoids the distraction of continuous note-taking.
- Confirming decisions in writing (especially where they may be disputed later) and taking agreed action.

Checklist of action

1. Wherever possible, speak then confirm in writing.
2. Establish systematic drills for: lateral contact; briefing and consultation.
3. Plan meetings, agendas and those attending with care.
4. Structure and control discussion, clarify decisions and action.
5. Follow up meetings to check action.
6. Prepare facts and location before interviews.
7. Get the interviewee to talk, and summarise discussions.
8. Confirm decisions in interviews and take agreed action.

4

EMPLOYEE RELATIONS

Using grievance and disciplinary procedures

Myths abound about law and procedures on employment. The simultaneous development of substantial employment legislation and the personnel function has made many line managers feel helpless in this field. This helplessness can be self-generating—the less managers use and understand procedures, the more the sphere of responsibility will be removed from them in practice. It is clearly nonsense to expect all line managers to become experts on employment law and procedures, but some understanding of the basic principles will help us to manage.

Understanding the principles

The first thing is to get hold of and read the procedure. Do not attempt to learn it by heart, but do check your limits of authority and what stages of procedure exist. Ideally, keep a copy available or at least know where to gain access to one.

Remember that discipline is about setting and maintaining standards, not taking punitive action. Make sure everyone understands the rules. Point out breaches informally and quickly. Use the first stages of procedure wherever possible, to clear the air and resolve the problem.

If using a formal procedure, take advice from the specialists but do not hand the problem over to them. We will have to manage the results of the grievance or disciplinary action, so we should be involved in the process.

Always get both sides of the story. We probably already

know our own view; the objective of an interviewer is to get the other person's.

If convinced we are right, we should be prepared to spend time and effort pushing a case all the way through the procedure.

Dismissal, though, is rare and extreme; the objective of using disciplinary procedure is to get behaviour or performance back to standard. It is only when we have failed to do this that further action should be contemplated.

Similarly, grievance procedure is there to put an area of concern into a system, where the complaint will be heard and possibly redressed. It is far better to use the procedure and thereby help solve problems, rather than sweeping them under the carpet.

Maintaining good relationships with trade unions

People tend to have strong political or social views on the role of trade unions. It is important for managers to put aside such views in favour of a much more pragmatic approach. Membership of trade unions at almost all levels of the public services is a fact. It is this fact that managers must live with and try to use constructively, rather than their own political desires. It is particularly important not to present other staff with an impression of confrontation and to co-operate where this is in the interests of the organisation and its staff. It is worth encouraging participation by all staff in their union's affairs as this will help to make unions more representative of the real views of the workforce.

Some important areas of action are:

- ensuring that union representatives understand their role and our attitude towards it
- introducing new staff to the appropriate union representative
- providing space on noticeboards for union activities

- understanding what agreed time and resources are allowed to union officials, and making sure that the agreement is kept to
- seeing newly-elected union representatives to make sure they understand the rules and our mutual roles
- encouraging joint training by management and unions for representatives, and encouraging attendance at such courses
- making sure that our own teams have management's views as well as that of the unions
- consulting union representatives at times of change, especially when terms and conditions may be affected
- ensuring that all grievance and discipline cases go to the first-line supervisor initially
- making all supervisors and managers aware of their precise responsibilities in grievance and discipline procedures
- making all staff clear about the rules.

Above all remember that trade union members and staff are one and the same set of people. There should, therefore, be a strong element of common interest and purpose between any organisation and its trade unions.

Checklist of action

1   Check discipline and grievance procedures and our own role within them.
2   Always check the facts and procedure and, if we need to, take advice before a disciplinary or grievance interview.
3   Set clear targets to get performance or behaviour back to standard. Monitor those targets.
4   Get to know union representatives and clarify the roles of manager and representative.
5   Encourage everybody to participate in union business.
6   Make sure that communication from management is at least as good as from the unions.

5

CONCLUSIONS

Further action to improve managerial effectiveness

The previous chapters represent a very brief attempt to highlight the important areas of action for public service managers in improving their effectiveness. There is no suggestion, of course, that they are all neglected at present. The intention is that an individual manager should be able to pick out areas which appear to be weak at the moment and work at those. We have to set ourselves targets and time-scales for these. Anyone can try to be a better manager. The person who succeeds is likely to have set themselves precise individual actions for getting there.

Most areas have been touched on rather than explored in detail. In particular, the concern has been to identify the drills: the systems and routines we must get into if we are to avoid perpetual crisis management. By recognising these responsibilities we can check to see if we are doing the job fully or not. Relatively little has been said about skills and the development of, for instance, interviewing and chairing skills. For some managers, further reading, training and practice will be required in these areas. In relation to both drills and skills, it is often helpful for managers to get together with colleagues of their own or of a mixture of disciplines, to work at a particular area under the leadership of an experienced and successful manager.

Deliberately, no reference has been made to two areas of concern to many public service managers: public account-ability and constraints on resources. As far as the latter is concerned it is, in the end, a matter for the electorate rather than officials. If, by managing more effectively, we save money that will serve some political objectives, equally it should enable us to provide better and more comprehensive services. Similarly, if we can demonstrate effectiveness to ourselves, we have the means to demonstrate it to the public and their elected representatives.

APPENDIX

EXAMPLES OF ACCOUNTABILITY CHARTS

a)

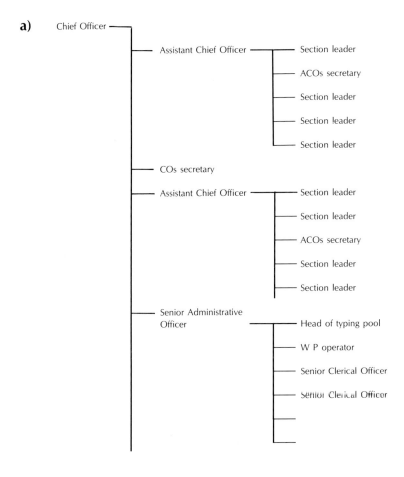

b)

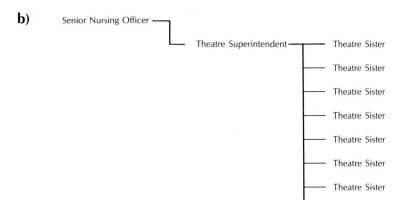

Senior Nursing Officer —

Theatre Superintendent —
- Theatre Sister
- Theatre Sister
- Theatre Sister
- Theatre Sister
- Theatre Sister
- Theatre Sister
- Theatre Sister
- Theatre Sister

c)

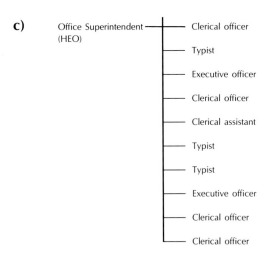

Office Superintendent (HEO) —
- Clerical officer
- Typist
- Executive officer
- Clerical officer
- Clerical assistant
- Typist
- Typist
- Executive officer
- Clerical officer
- Clerical officer

Note: names should be entered in alphabetical order.